The
Power
OF
American Women

THE *Power* OF *American Women*

DR. FRANÇOIS ADJA ASSEMIEN

Ordering Information:

For orders and inquiries, please contact:
1-888-404-1388
www.goldtouchpress.com
book.orders@goldtouchpress.com

Printed in the United States of America

CONTENTS

FROM THE SAME AUTHOR

- The African Rebels, novel, Page Turner, 2020
- The Golden Rules of Personal Success, Health, Happiness and Salvation, Edilivre, 2016
- Introduction to philocure, essay, Edilivre, 2016
- Forbidden Africa, novel, Edilivre, 2016
- The World is worth nothing, essay, Edilivre, 2016
- Côte d'Ivoire hurts, essay, Edilivre, 2018
- The Current slavery in Africa, essay, Global Summit House 2000
- The way to live in America, guide, Edilivre, 2019
- Moral and spiritual education, manual, Edilivre, 2016
- The African Consciousness, essay, Edilivre, 2016
- Thomas Sankara as Thomas More and Socrate, essay, Ouagadoudou, 2020
- Ahikaba, novel, Mary Bro Foundation Publishing, London, 2018
- Electoral Code, novel, Black Stars, 1995
- Portrait of the good and the bad voter, of the good and the bad candidate, essay, Black Stars, 2000
- Côte d'Ivoire with its foreigners, essay, Black Stars, 2002
- Political Thought to Save Côte d'Ivoire, essay, Afro-Star, 2003

- The African Guide to Philosophy, Human Sciences and Humanism, Abidjan, 1985
- Afrocratism, essay, Afro-star, 2003

- Corona virus, essay, Global Summit House, 2000
- Let's save humanity and life, essay, Global Summit House, 2021

INTRODUCTION

I am going to give here my testimony on the American women that I see and rub shoulders with every day in America. I will say things that I see and observe on a daily basis. I am going to play my role of sociologist and philosopher in front of a very important societal phenomenon that is the woman in a very special country. I do this job to educate the outside world that ignores American realities. I report on my human, social, psychological, political, economic, cultural experience and environment. With my eyes as a foreigner and an African living in another world, I discover beings, things, realities that cannot leave me indifferent. I am very sensitive to everything I see and hear every day. My daily life in America is a school for me. It gives me precious lessons that I want to share with all those who may be interested in it (researchers, thinkers, ordinary people, and curious people).

I admit that America is fascinating for the foreigners who discover it. An African who stays in America sees far too many amazing things that he would never have imagined being in Africa. People, societies, mentalities, cultures and civilizations around the world are very different from each other. To find out, you have to travel, to leave your native country, to go and meet others. You have to go and study others, to live with them, to get to know them. Generally, it is Westerners who do this by staying elsewhere, very far from their countries, especially in Africa. They are academically called ethnologists, anthropologists. Thus Louis-Vincent Thomas (French philosopher) studied the people of Casamance in Senegal. The French monk Vincent Guerry studied the Baoule of Côte d'Ivoire. Father Tempels (Belgian) studied the Bantu (Bantu **philosophy**). French philosopher Fernand Lafargue studied the Abidji of Côte d'Ivoire. The French man Alain Gracias, professor of Latin and French, studied the language of the Gwa people of Côte d'Ivoire. I was his student and his interpreter with the Gwa. I belong to this tribe.

It is very rare that African intellectuals write books or theses on Western peoples. Why? Because they are assimilated to Westerners (colonization obliges). They are westernized and therefore they have no particular curiosity with regard to western mores, customs, cultures and civilizations. African thinkers, researchers, ethnologists, sociologists, anthropologists and psychologists study their own African realities. For example, the Ivorian professor Georges Niangoran Bouah wrote: "Introduction to drumology". The Senegalese professor Assane Sylla wrote: "The moral philosophy of the Wolof". Professor Cheickh Anta Diop wrote: "The cultural unity of black Africa", "Negro nations and culture". This means that I am sailing against the current. I am starting a new business by writing this book on America. It's a kind of Copernican revolution. It is a historical work. I am thus opening a door to Africans. This will undoubtedly allow them to change their intellectual and academic habits.

Finally, this book comes out of the gaze of a curious and admiring African who compares America to his country (Côte d'Ivoire) and to his continent. He compares the American female junta to that elsewhere. This book strongly emphasizes the difference between America and Africa. He invites African women to imitate the exemplary nature of American women. This exemplary nature of American women constitutes a world school. This school teaches women the secrets and rules of power, happiness, dignity, prosperity and success.

AMERICAN WOMEN'S OMNIPRESENCE

Women are depressed and dominated by men in most countries in the world. It is obvious. I am talking about physical, political, economic, social, cultural, intellectual, spiritual domination. Weakness and helplessness are imposed as virtues on women from birth by phallocratic or patriarchal societies. It is part of his family and societal education. It is enshrined in the habits and customs of African and Eastern countries. The opposite is true in America. Indeed, this country offers an exceptional policy concerning women. Let's call it the **omnipresence of women.** This is a very striking phenomenon for an African foreigner in America. It is also a very pleasant sight for this African foreigner. He has the feeling that America is only inhabited by women. He feels like women have all the power in their hands in America. Indeed, women are very visible everywhere, in all public and private services, in all activities of the country and at all levels. Nothing is forbidden to them. They are worthily and admirably present in all fields.

Women everywhere occupy and exercise very high positions in general administration, public administration, in the formal and informal sectors. They are present in a preponderant way in all places of work and leisure. They are used in all shops, all supermarkets, all restaurants, all offices, all hospitals, all schools, and all universities. They drive buses, taxis, trains, planes... The American population (300,000,000 inhabitants) is very strongly feminized. Uncle Sam's country is almost entirely populated by women. It belongs to women. America is dominated and managed by women. Today, the post of Vice-President is assigned to a woman named Kamala Harris. I have done all of the most physical and difficult jobs: landscaping, construction, demolition, cleaning, driving, delivering. These jobs are normally and generally performed by men in other countries, especially in African countries. But here, in America, I have met women challenging men. They were my colleagues (coworkers). What feminine bravery! What feminine courage! What feminine power! Well done to the women!

America merges with women. It is defined by women. Women make America. Elsewhere, especially in African countries, life and all things it involves are in the hands of men alone. Men are numerically superior to women in all workplaces, in all social, professional and economic activities. They hold everything in their hands and manage the whole continent on their own. They have a monopoly on everything. They are omnipresent and omnipotent. They are gods. Political, economic, cultural, intellectual, social, spiritual life is under their total control and absolute domination. They have a monopoly on initiative and action. They are the undisputed absolute masters of Africa.

It deserves to be detailed. Africa is politically masculinized. In general, only men are Presidents, Heads of State, Vice-Presidents, Ministers, Representatives, Senators, Prime Ministers, Central Directors, Directors General (Liberia and Ethiopia excepted). My opponents will cite a few African countries where there are women ministers, representatives, directors... But these are the exceptions which confirm the rule. These few exceptional women are stooges. Their number is very derisory or symbolic. These reckless and rebellious female politicians who brave men are drops of water in the ocean. The ocean is the overwhelming number of men who absolutely rule over women. Indeed, the Presidents of all the important institutions are men: Supreme Court, Economic and Social Council, Senate, National Assembly, Prefects, Sub-Prefects, Mayors, Chiefs of Staff of the armed forces.

In the field of economics, too, there is the primacy of man, the absolute domination of man over woman. Indeed, all the major players, investors and creators of businesses, factories and plantations (employers) are men.

The economy is the monopoly, the prerogative and the exclusive privilege of men. Women play supporting roles, the roles of subordinates. They are used by men. They are not employers. They totally lack weight and economic strength in front of men. They are passive and not active. They are dependent on men. Economic strength and power belong to men in Africa. African men also practice their domination over women in the cultural and intellectual field. This is very visible. Thus in schools, universities and research institutes, we generally and especially see men. Most of the teacher, researchers and professors are men. It's the same thing in hospitals, the military, the police and elsewhere. Women are rare in working life in Africa. It is quite the opposite in America. American women are present in all centers of decision, action and responsibility. They are superior to men in number and equal to men in output and skill. In African countries, are there how many women doctors, professors, engineers, police officers, soldiers, lawyers, magistrates, scientists, technicians, writers, philosophers distinguished and awarded (the Nobel Prize)? This quality of woman is in plethora in America. There lies the yawning gulf that separates Africa from America. One country dominates an entire continent.

African women must break with immobility, laziness, cowardice, weakness and the taste for ease. They must stop being pitiful and lagging behind men. They must now struggle and free themselves from male domination and oppression. They must gain their independence, their sovereignty, their dignity and power. Who does not fight remains mediocre, small, inferior, miserable, unhappy, unworthy, irresponsible, weak, slave, ashamed. The African women must stop playing babies, beggars, the incapable. This is not the common sense of life. Life is meant to be a ruthless and deadly fight. It is a war of all against all that everyone must win. You win it or you disappear. It is a balance of power. It is the law of the jungle or the law of the strongest. You dominate or you are dominated. You are victorious or you are vanquished. You are a master or you are a slave. It is the great ruthless competition for happiness, power, domination. If African women understand this and change their minds, all will be well for them and for Africa. They will dare to use their Reason and their will to power that lie dormant in them. They will challenge the phallocratic and misogynistic prejudices of the Bible and the Koran. They will shake, awaken and activate their higher faculties which make better and higher beings, great men and great women. They will thus remake their history and their destiny. Africa desperately awaits their omnipresence, their omnipotence and their omniscience. "Women, you can. Just do it".

AMERICAN WOMEN AND WORK

America can be defined by this expression: "union, discipline, work" which is the national motto of Côte d'Ivoire. The word that interests us the most here is "Work". What does mean work? What is its value for the individual and for a country? Work consists in rendering service to the world, in producing, creating goods, things that are useful for life, for humanity. It is based on physical effort and intelligence. It is about spending physical or mental energy. The utilitarian activity of one and the other based on morality and law constitutes work. Workers, teachers, engineers, doctors, lawyers, judges, planters or farmers, traders, laborers, police officers, guards, journalists, pilots work. Work is opposed to leisure, to disinterested activity, to rest. It brings in a gain (salary). Voltaire said: "Work takes away from us three great evils: boredom, want and vice". This is verifiable in America. Indeed, it is through hard work that America was created and developed rapidly. America owes its economic prosperity, its spectacular success, peace, security, its immense wealth, extraordinary power, incredible greatness and its happiness to the work accomplished night and day by its tireless and brave men and women.

America lives and depends on the toil of its population which is numerically dominated by women. It must be said here that women are the pride, the greatness, the strength, the honor and the power of America. Indeed, America is the result of the work of its intrepid women who work very courageously and without respite. The American women are not sparing their strength and their efforts. They are one hundred percent in the social and economic battle. They are present in all socio-economic activities. They hold almost everything in their hardworking, creative, helpful, daring hands. They are at the head of services and businesses of all kinds. They manage them very well. They are very competent. They produce, manufacture and sell everything that allows America to live in honor, dignity, glory, superabundance, opulence. Women's work is absolutely profitable. Women are an abundant and efficient workforce. Their overwhelming number in every service, every job, every function and every trade is saving America and its economy. Their rigor, their seriousness and their sense of discipline at work are very admirable and beneficial. It makes America happy, powerful.

To the foreigner and the observer I am, women are the true symbol or the best emblem of America. Women are America's torchbearers. They are America's workhorse, shield, economic fortress. Without the invaluable contribution of women, America would lack splendor, power, grandeur, beauty, any capacity to meet its political, economic, social, cultural and historical challenges. Women are the womb or the foster mother of America. They embodie the fundamental and primary economic and social value of America. They are the heart, the lungs and the engine of the socio-economic life of America. They have received the appropriate and necessary training to enable them to play this vital role. They have great diplomas and they are very professionally qualified. They are very deserving. They are free and sovereign. They are not controlled, dominated, alienated, discriminated by men. Phallocracy is fought, condemned. Women and men are equal in everything. They are equal in rights and dignity. Both are doomed to earn their daily bread by the sweat of their brow. Besides that American women give birth in pain, they suffer socially (through labor) by earning their bread. They suffer a double suffering. They are doubly powerful thanks to motherhood and social work. This makes America the world's leading power. Glory goes to American women.

What can we say about women elsewhere, especially African women? Do they make the greatness, the strength, the power, the honor and the glory of their countries? No. Why? There are several reasons for this. The main reason is that African countries practice phallocracy, discrimination and exclusion of women. In Africa, there is no coherent, rational, legitimate and adequate policy for the integration of women into social, economic, political, cultural, intellectual, school, academic or national life. Women are generally marginalized, neglected and forbidden to act, think and do a lot of things in Africa. The habits and customs and the mentality of Africans are responsible for that. Officially, the African women do not have a status which allows them to impose themselves on the men. They are neglected, left to their own devices. The phallocratic societies do not take their defense. They do nothing to help women progress. On the contrary, they push women down and keep them weak and helpless. The state gives priority and primacy to man. The state is masculinized. It is misogynist. It encourages, organizes and promotes the domination, contempt and endless oppression of women by men (abuse, domestic violence). African customs and cultures sanction the inferiorization, submission, discrimination and marginalization of women (phallocracy). Men are considered as the absolute and exclusive heads of the families, as the kings of the women. It is they alone who do the hard jobs and wage war. Women play supporting roles alongside them. They take care of the housework. Their official and historic place is in the kitchen. They cook for their families, maintain, raise and educate their children. They are married very young, from their puberty. They are especially intended to found a marital home and to have children. They are deprived of the right to study for a long time in countries where girls are still allowed to go to school. Their schooling is cut short in favor of marriage (forced or arranged marriage).

Consequently, they can neither be qualified nor graduated to exercise honorable trades or professions worthy of national interest. All important, serious, political, economic, military and other jobs are intended for men. Women are rare in the public service. They are not wrestlers who can break their chains as dominated persons, excluded by men in power at all high levels of society. They do not have the right to speak in most situations. The right to work, to participate in public affairs, in political, intellectual and scientific life is practically, directly or indirectly denied to them. They are treated as fragile, shabby, inferior, unintelligent, incompetent and irresponsible. Women are assimilated to children and confined to house to play only the roles of mothers, wives, housewives, educators. And they are very proud of it. A proverb says: "If a woman raises a sheep, it is a man who sets the price for sale". It means that only men are intelligent, competent, responsible and able to do all serious, important things successfully and happily. Women are contemptible, unworthy and ashamed. When we want to despise or humiliate a man, we treat him as a woman. He is compared to a woman. They say he is a woman and not a man. Indeed, it is men who must make all the decisions. It is men who make the laws. And women obey it.

In addition, laxity, laziness, cheating and the taste for ease are set up in laws in Africa. Everyone practices these things. They are considered normal and legitimate. So what can we blame women who do not fight against these national defects and vices? Are the African women to blame if they are the opposite of the American women? No. The political, sociological and historical context explains and justifies their character, their lack of dynamism, of a sense of aristocratic responsibility (Nietzsche). They are in accordance with the order and the socio-political and historical system in force in their countries. They are disciplined, civilized, humanized and moralized by their countries. There is a saying: "every river has the caimans it deserves". This means that each country manufactures its citizens to its liking and needs. It is a matter of paradigm, custom, tradition, culture and civilization. The African women are then within their rights, duties and roles. They are the image of their societies. Their countries are built on a stinking and heavily infected trash can. If the general condition of their countries changes and improves, they too can change and improve. They and their countries are merged and form one and the same entity. There is a dialectical relationship between the two. Indeed, society determines individual and, conversely, individual determines society. There is interdependence or mutual conditioning between the African women and their countries. Africans must make their own revolution. They must create the "United, Disciplined and Dynamic States of Africa"!

THE BEAUTY OF AMERICAN WOMEN

Physical beauty is a natural gift of American women. Physical beauty is difficult to define. Because there is no universal or conventional way to measure the beauty of every woman. Physical beauty has no universal model. There is no beauty in itself as an absolute corresponding to the taste of everyone on earth. All our personal judgments which qualify some women as beautiful and others as ugly are therefore arbitrary, subjective, unconventional. Each human being sees the others as he is and not as the others are. Value judgments are all subjective and relative. Tastes and appreciations vary from one individual to another. One thing can please me and not please others. We are all different from each other. Our tastes too are different. I can say that a woman named Mary is beautiful while others find her ugly. The criteria of appreciation or evaluation of the beauty of women vary according to the peoples, the societies, the individuals. It is related to culture and education. An adage rightly says: "Tastes and colors, we must not discuss them". Everyone is right. There is no universal consensus or absolute truth on this subject. It depends on our personal fantasies, our visions or conceptions of things coming from our education which is based on our cultural values.

That being said, my appreciation for the beauty of American women may be challenged or approved by others. I love American women. I find them very beautiful. A question arises. Is it because American women are very beautiful that I love them or is it because I love them that I find them very beautiful? It is undoubtedly the two situations. I contemplate American women every day and everywhere. Their bodies and styles stir my soul. That gives me pleasure, joy, happiness. How to describe American women? American female population is very diverse. It includes several ethnicities or races. There are whites, blacks, mestizos, yellows, reds. All races, ethnicities, peoples and the products of their crossbreeds exist in America. It is very pleasant to see. The color or complexion of American women is generally very charming, attractive. I also like their shapes. Some American women are tall, slender, (White Caucasians). Others are of medium height with a dark or chocolate complexion. They are thin, refined. They are Ethiopians, Somalis, Eritreans, Hindus, Guineans, Fulani. Others are small, fat or thin, white or red (Latino and American Indian).

In reality, things are very complex. The physical features are very difficult to describe. The interbreeding or biological mixture of races and peoples from all parts of the world has produced strange, special, fantastic beings. The color of the eyes, the shape of the nose, the complexion, the length and the quality of the hair and others of the people are fascinating. It makes American women very attractive. To have this result, America had to welcome all the races and peoples of earth to its soil. So xenophobic countries are wrong. A country which refuses foreigners on its soil has a very big shortfall on all fronts. It is necessarily poor and weak. Because foreigners bring new values and wealth of all kinds. They are the source of happiness, greatness, power, success, beauty and prosperity. Foreigners create history. They contribute to progress, to qualitative and quantitative development. America teaches us this lesson. It made the best choice. The cultural, civilizational and biological mixing gives excellent products, excellent fruits which make the beauty and the power of societies open to the outside world. This enriches countries and improves the quality of their men, women and populations.

Regarding the criteria defining the physical beauty of women, the African society from which I come has retained certain values or qualities. With us, the Akans of Ivory Coast, in particular the sub-group called Gwa, a woman is qualified as beautiful if she possesses the following qualities: tall or medium height, complexion either fair, or black, or tanned, or chocolatey, pointed or aquiline nose, very white teeth, lot of natural hair, fullness or thinness, large breasts or medium breasts straightened, large buttocks or medium buttocks, wide pelvis or medium pelvis, large calves or medium calves, long striated neck. Man, who wants to marry a woman, takes these qualities into account. He chooses his ideal bride based on this. If his wife does not meet most of these conditions described, he will be unhappy. Because he will be the laughing stock of everyone. He will be insulted, despised and humiliated. He will be called a rascal, a sucker, a fool, an individual without good taste. He will shame his friends, his parents, his comrades. His marriage could die of it. It will be a failure.

AMERICAN WOMEN AND KNOWLEDGE

One can establish an inclusive link between beauty, knowledge and moral good. For Plato, these three things are inseparable. A being said to be beautiful is a being who has beautiful ideas. Beautiful ideas constitute true knowledge. The being who has true knowledge is beautiful and good. For the ancient Greeks, to be beautiful is also to be good and knowing. Beauty necessarily goes with goodness and truth. The beauty of the body translates the beauty of the spirit (true, certain knowledge) and goodness (moral perfection). We called the American women beautiful. Are they also knowledgeable, learned, well-made and full heads?

Unlike other countries where most women are illiterate, America makes it a point of honor to educate, train its women. America has given itself this as its sacred duty, as a national obligation, as its sovereign task. All American girls therefore have the right and the duty to go to school. They are all educated. They are in all areas of knowledge. They have pure or theoretical knowledge, practical, technical or professional knowledge and interpersonal skills. They receive government grants or elsewhere to study in large and prestigious universities like Harvard, Yale... They are in all subjects which lead to various, noble and very profitable trades. This is, for example, the profession of lawyer, judge, professor, engineer, researcher, doctor etc. The list of American intellectuals, scholars, writers and thinkers is immeasurable. Let's see it in detail.

When it comes to philosophy, America has a plethora of female philosophers. Thus Angela Davis, Bell Hooks, Judith Butler, Gayatri Spivak, Chandra Talpade Mohanty, Wendy Brown, Maria Lugones, Katharine Mackinnon, Sally Haslanger, Talia Mae Bettcher, Gloria Anzaldua, Judith Jarvis Thomson, Hortense Spillers, Kathryn Sophia belle, Martha Nussbaum, Ruth Barcan Marcus, Lory Janelle dance, Donna Haraway, Andrea Dworkin, Patricia Churchland, Lisa Delpit. This list is not exhaustive. The main and common object of study of these philosophers is the conflicting relationship between man and woman, sexism (phallocracy and feminism). All these great philosophers thought and fought for justice, equality, independence, freedom, dignity, happiness in favor of American women. They defended the cause and the rights of women in American society. They are vigilantes and theorists like Simone de Beauvoir, in France, author of **The Second Sex.** Their figurehead or iconic figure is activist Angela Davis (torchbearer). It is the most popular. She is the legend, the icon of American feminism as an ideologue and revolutionary guide.

When it comes to literature, America is full of very talented women and distinguished writers. The list of these is impressive. Here are the names of a few: Toni Morrison, Carson Mc Cullers, Sylvia Plath, Gertrude Stein, Pearl S. Buck, Harper Lee, Joyce Carol Oates, Willa Cather, Flannery O'Connor, Siri Hustvedt, Margaret Michell, Laura Kasischke, Patricia Highsmith, Barbara Kingsolver, Lois MoMaster, Suzy Beker, Elizabeth Graeme Fer, Laura Ingallls

Wild, Edith Wharton, Louise Erdrich, Mary Higgins Cla, Jennifer Winkley, Lee Holleman Mc Carthy, Annie Delisle.

Now here are the names of the most famous American women scientists: Diane Fossey, Vera Rubin, Sally Ride, Nettie Stevens, Richel Louise Carson, Stephanie Kwolek, Nancy Dupree, Marge Champion, Elinor Ostrom, Linda Nochlin, Mildred Dresselhaus, Lioudmila Alexeeva.

Here is the list of women Nobel Prize winners: Jennifer Doudna, Andrea Ghez, Emily Greene Balch, Jane Addhams, Louise Glück, Maria Goeppert Mayer, Barbara Mc Clintock, Gerty Theresa Cori, Gertrude Elion, Linda B. Buck, Carol Greider.

The American women astronauts are: Christina Koch, Jessica Meir, Sally Ride, Mae Carol Jemison, Kalpana Chawla, Anousheh Ansari, Sunita Williams, Eileen M. Collins, Anne Mc Clain, Peggy Whitson, Kathryn D. Sullivan, Judith Resnik, Christa McAuliffe, Anna Lee Fisher, Ellen Ochoa, Stephanie Wilson, Jasmin Moghbeli, Jessica Watkins, Shannon Lucid, Kathleen Rubins, Kayla

Barron, Nicole Aunapu Ma, Jan Davis, Shannon Walker, Tracey Caldwell Dy, Kathry P. Hire, Serena Aunon-Cha, K. Megan McArthur, Jeanette Epps, Zena Cardman, Bonnie J. Dunbar, Marsha Ivins, Susa Helms, Janice E. Voss, Kathryn C. Thornton, Tamara E. Jernigan, Margaret Rhea Sedd, Nicole Stott, Laurel Clark, Dorothy Metcalf-lin, Pamela Melrog, Loral O'Hara, Lisa Nowak, Barbara Morgan, Catherine Colman, Karen Nyberg, Joan Higginboth, Heidemarie Stefanyshyn-Piper, Nancy J. Currie-Gregg, **Katherine Johnson**, Kitty O'Brien Joyner (Engineer at NASA), Dorothy Vaughan (first African- American head of NASA), **Mary Jackson** (first black woman engineer at NASA. It is called human computer), Nancy Roman (first chief astronomer at NASA), **Christine Koch.**

Women airplane pilots are very numerous. Let us quote a few of them. Amelia Earhart, Jacqueline Cochran, Nancy Harkness L., Elizabeth L. Gardner, Rosemary Bryant Mari, Jerrie Cobb, Blanche Noyes, Shaesta Waiz, Florence Klingensmith, Meryl Getline, Deanie Parrish, Bessie Colman, Phoebe Omlie, Betty Gillies, Elinor Smith, Eileen Collins, Michelle Curran, Jerrie Mock, Harriet Quimby, Dora Dougherly, Evelyn Sharp, Ruth Law Oliver, Barbara Erickson Lo, Marge Hurlburt, Gertrude Tompkings, Rosa Charlyne Cr, Dorothy Olsen, Sara Payne Hayden, Anne Noggle, Margeret Rigenberg, Hazen Yin Lee, Cornelia Fort, Martha McSally, Rosemary Bryant Mari, Ruth Rowland Ni, Marjorie Stinson, Katherine Stinson, Bonnie Tiburzi, Shaesta Waiz, Shawna Rochelle Ki, Blanche Scott, Nelli Zabel Willhite, Jerrie Cobb, Aida de Acosta, Louise Thaden, Anne Morrow Lin, Pancho Barnes, Alys Mckey Bryant, Mary Barr, Beverly Burns, Vicki Van Meter, Bessie Raiche, Emily Howell War, Willa Brown, Azellia White.

These American women are heroines. They challenged the men. They piloted space ships, fighter planes and airliners. At this level, let's dream a little. When will each African country also have its women pilots? Are African women brave, daring, fearless? No. They are not trained, educated to be. They are marginalized, neglected, ignored in all activities that are glorious, dangerous or at very high risk. The activities that are very serious or at risk are reserved to men in Africa. Indeed, men are regarded as the holder of exclusive, absolute power, intelligence, courage, wisdom. Thus they alone can and must study, graduate and do business that is difficult, perilous. They are omnipresent, omniscient and omnipotent. They are chiefs or kings everywhere. They are the masters of the world. They are the supreme authority instituted by God (Bible, Koran) in the world. So they are feared, respected, admired and loved by women. Women need their kindness. Men are invincible and invulnerable warriors. They are infallible, perfect. Even a baby boy is seen as such by women and society. He is educated and prepared to play this role, to embody and express this supreme value. But the baby girl, meanwhile, is educated and prepared to obey the man when she is a grown woman, and a wife. Man is thought and manufactured man. Woman is thought and made woman by phallocratic and patriarchal society.

In Africa, it is said that a girl sent to school only serves to nothing. We are very skeptical and very pessimistic about the nature and value of women. Women are very despised, very underestimated. They are minimized. Thus we confine all the girls at home and we make them play the roles of wives, mothers and housewives. That is their only utility. So they say society, nature and God want it. All the little girls and all the women and mothers have internalized this vision in their subconscious, in their minds. In Africa, women's essential attributes are weakness, powerlessness, inferiority, submission, limitation, inability, irresponsibility, love of ease, fear, laziness. Women are conceived as beings that are made to cry, to be dominated, to implore pity, kindness, condescension, kindness, generosity, affection and love of man. They are represented as big babies, beggars.

African Women see themselves as weak, incompetent, irresponsible, as beings which must absolutely depend on the men to satisfy all their needs and make a living. Women see men as their shields, their fortress, their covers, their protectors, their defenders, their ramparts, the guarantors of their safety and their life. In such a context, it is impossible to make women scientists, engineers, pilots, astronauts, scientists, senior technicians capable of exercising all the trades of this world. It is absolutely impossible to have women who make their countries powerful, rich, prosperous, beautiful, independent, free, worthy, sovereign. The African view of women is diametrically opposed to the American view of women. Women are not emancipated in Africa as it is in America. The African women do not take responsibility, do not assert themselves, do not struggle. They are chained and dominated by the complexes of inferiority, helplessness and weakness. So they can not contribute to the development of their countries. As for American women, they are free from any negative complex. They are victorious warriors. They know how to fight, to impose themselves, to assert themselves. America has deleted the difference between men and women. Women are equal to men. The condescending phallocracy is killed.

AMERICAN WOMEN
AND MORALS

The ancient Greeks said that being beautiful is being very good, vertuous in the same time (kalos agathos). Beauty goes with kindness and ugliness goes with malice. Beauty equals good, kindness and ugliness equals evil. In other words, physical beauty is the expression of moral, intellectual, mental, psychological beauty (beauty of ideas, of thoughts). To think well is to act well. It is to behave well towards others. It is to be virtuous, good. There is therefore an adequacy of the body with the mind and with the personal conduct in life. We said American women are beautiful, charming, seductive, sublime. In the Greek or Platonic sense, this means that they are also moral, virtuous. Morals is, in general, a discipline that teaches ideal conduct to humanity. It defines us good and evil. It imposes good on us and forbids us from evil. It is embodied in customs, in traditions, in law, in religious and political rules. It is relative. Each country or people has its own morals or morality. He who complies with the morality or morals of his country is said virtuous, wise, good, civilized, patriot, loyalist. He is a correct moral agent. Whoever violates the moral rules of his country is said immoral. He is wild, barbaric, undisciplined. In principle, he is unacceptable in society. He is banished, imprisoned, punished. He may even deserve death, that is to say death penalty. Is America lax, careless, tolerant of its immoral, unruly, harmful citizens? Does America allow people to hurt? No. America is a very well organized and well governed society. It is very repressive regarding evil. America is not a can of worms where each crab hurts at most other crabs with its dangerous claws. America is not a jungle where each devours the other according to his strength. America is a society of law, of morals and of religion (In God we trust). All Americans are disciplined to the max. They are submissive and obedient to the legal law, to the moral law and to religious law. None can resist it. There is no place for anarchists, nihilists and outlaws in America. All the land of Uncle Sam is absolutely secure and protected by its police omnipresent and omnipotent.

We know, from Socrates, that no one is wicked voluntarily and that only by **ignorance** humans are evil to their neighbors. The American women are well educated, cultured, civilized. They have received the rules of politeness, courtesy, respect and love of neighbor. They are dominated by humanism, civility and patriotism. They are very enlightened and calm. They are not under the yoke of ignorance, a factor of evil according to Socrates. They are held in respect by the forces of order and public security. It is said that the fear of the police officer is the beginning of wisdom. This means that humans do good by duress. They refrain from doing harm by duress. American society and American women are human creatures. They reflect the power of men. Society is imagined and invented by men. Its progress, its development, its values, its functions, its objectives and its ends are thought out and rethought by man. It is the daily work of man as an individual and as a group. Thus man and society are always becoming, in permanent instability. We can not freeze, close, limit anything. Evolution is our nature. We are beings who are defined by evolution, progress, development. We are history. We are thus opposed to the beast which has a closed nature, completed, limited by nature. human being is freedom. We own contradictions and contradictions make us evolve, grow. So we are perfectible. We are capable of anything, capable of both good and bad. We are capable of better and of worse. Man is elusive, indefinable. He is both the best and the worst beings that are in the universe. He is both dominated and dominator, weak and powerful. He is a thinking reed, said Blaise Pascal. "Reed" means his weakness and "thinking" means his power. So man makes rain and shine. He is the measure of everything according to sophist Protagoras. We can see that today. We see what he's capable of. He destroyed ascetic morality and distorted politics which is the means of achieving ascetic morality. And devil has taken over the world. Think about covid-19. Consider the Luciferian and satanic project called the "new world order" in the course of implementation very accelerated. Let us think about all actions of the Free masons, Illuminati and globalists. The whole world and civilization are in danger of disappearing. Who can save us? Who can we count on? What is our lifeline? Such are the painful questions to ask today face to all threats and to all tragedies.

We are carried away by the tragic morals of the powerful and the masters of darkness. Nietzsche laughs and Marx cries. Nietzsche triumphs over Marx. Both thinkers as authors and influencers of history are still alive and very powerful. The devil is in front of the good Lord. The duel is very exacerbated. It is at its peak. The devil is out of the shadows and showed his true face openly to the world. His disciples are in action to realize its full level against humanity. These times are very serious. Times are no longer for games but for the third world war. "We are at war," says Emmanuel Macron. It is the war of the creation of a terrifying mess and a deadly world abusively called the "new world order". "Nobody can escape", says Nicola Sarkozi, a former French President. It is about extermination, criminal domination, total control, absolute oppression, cynical exploitation of all the weak by the powerful world capitalists. The following facts speak for: jobs destruction, muzzling or compulsory wearing of face masks, physical distancing, mass killing, planetary genocide, biochemical terrorism, spraying, depopulation of the world, villainous, sterilant, deadly vaccines, gene therapy, dictatorship, totalitarianism, absolutism, monstrous despotism and fascism. It is Apocalypse. "The Beast is in", says Emmanuel Macron. It is the most criminal and generalized barbarism on earth. It is roughly the creation of a demonic, collectivist, dynastic and tyrannical world government that will confiscate all the goods and all the riches of earth, all human rights and all freedoms in the hands of predators, racists, eugenics, slavers, imperialists and terrorists with the means of the UN, the World Bank, the WHO, the IMF, NATO etc. A lot of things need to be said here: single digital currency, preventing from human attachment, marriage, procreation. There will be cloning, robotics, human zombification, drastic reduction of the population of earth, earth cooling, control of every human thanks to electronic chips put in everyone's body, 5 G...).

Here is the place to ask American women who are known for their bravery, heroism and their strong fighting spirit in history to rise as a single individual to stop all unheard crimes against humanity (Covid-19, new world order) and prevent a catastrophic third world war that is on the horizon. It is about saving ascetic morals, civilization and humanity in deadly danger. American women, you can play this glorious and beneficial role. You have already proved this ability in American history. This is your historic mission. I trust you. Yes, you can. Just do it.

AMERICAN WOMEN AND POLITICS

Politics is the realization of morals, that is to say ascetic values in the world. It is the instrument that each country uses to create its happiness or the common good. The end of national politics is **good** (Aristotle). The national politics consists in creating the just and wholesome order and the conditions of freedom to the development and progress of the people. That appeals to ideal notions like republic, democracy, state etc. Modern times have adopted a these ideals as universal models or paradigms. The whole world now swears by these political notions. Countries go to war over it. All nations are judged and compared to each other with respect to their progress and degree in the realization of democracy, republic, State. Each country tries to do better than the others. Everyone wants to be world champion in politics. And each nation makes it a point of honor to try to realize the ideals of democracy, republic and state otherwise it will disappear from the world. It will be attacked and destroyed by its competitors, that is to say the powerful and imperialists countries. Every small country must give its political results to the Community of masters and world powerful (UN). Watch out for the last one in the world ranking! Attention to one that does not the desire to the UN! The latter does not have the right to live. It will be beheaded by the UN-NATO (Libya, Yugoslavia, Romania, Côte d'Ivoire, Burkina Faso, Mali, Guinea, Ghana, Togo, Congo...).

The political question joins the moral question. Indeed, politics is subject to ascetic morals. It is controlled by ascetic morals. Its foundation is this morals. Otherwise, it does not make sens and has no raison to exist. Because the politicians have to fight for the good and the happiness of the people. Politics is the way to organize civil society, to make it live and function by providing it with effective institutions and structures. So politics has to solve the economic and social problem. It has to produce goods and wealth (economy) and to share that with citizens (social problem). Politics is an action which results in a relationship of power, that is to say a relationship between dominant and dominated (Julien Freund). Rulers or leaders make laws and their subjects obey them. Politics consists in governing or ruling a country. Politicians decide everyone's fate, choose the ideal values for the citizens. Their responsibility is to keep things under control, to make justice, peace, security in society, to defend the common interests, freedom and to promote prosperity, morality, virtue. The modern state is the government of man through legal law. This law is the expression of the general will. So obedience to the law is obedience to oneself, to oneself reasonable willingness. It is not to be dominated, alienated but to be free and responsible. This is the meaning of republican and democratic politics. This is why men prefer the democratic and republican regime. Democracy is defined as "government of the people by the people and for the people" (Abraham Lincoln). In any case, it is the political system in which the people govern themselves either directly or through representatives chosen by themselves for their freedom and happiness. It is the family regime according to the philosopher Alain.

As for Republic, it is opposed to monarchy, that is to say the system of kings (kingship). Europe has known the absolute monarchy of divine right (France). It was abandoned because of its vices and cruelty that are unbearable. Its opposite, republic, does a lot of good. Republic means public affairs, that is to say politics that defends the common interest, which benefits to all citizens (the common good). Republic thus joins democracy. In republic, it is everyone (the people) who governs society while in monarchy, it is only one (the king) who governs the whole country. America has practiced the democratic system since its inception. But the executive power is always held and exercised mainly by male junta. Here is my problem. Up to now, only men are Presidents in America. I hope that women too will one day exercise executive power, that they will be Presidents. Women must henceforth be Presidents of the United States of America. Why? In chapters earlier, I showed the American women's value, talent, skill, merits. Women make America. They are highly qualified professionally, intellectually and morally. They are very brave. Their sense of humanism, patriotism and civility is highly developed. They are very virtuous. They perform very well everywhere. They are heroines. They have physical, intellectual and moral beauty. They make America prosperous, successful, greater, powerful, glorious. Currently, America's Vice President is a woman. It is already beautiful but insufficient. Women deserve more. They deserve the **presidency.** They are origin of life. They know better than men the value of the human being that they bring into the world. They know what is the cost of nine months of pregnancy and the cost of the fact of giving birth to a baby. They are willing to die to bring man to the world. They **love humanity.** They practice **self-denial** or **self-sacrifice.** They are saints, renunciators. They are thus guarantees of pure ascetic morals which is currently in danger of death. Politics is no longer the realization of perfect morals. It is rather the enemy of pure morals. Only women can save **pure morals** and **pure politics.** We must therefore give them political power so that they save humanity, civilization and the world. They must be given supreme power so that they preserve human life that demons, wizards and mystics of all stripes (globalists and eugenics) are currently slaughtering and destroying. In their moral and natural role, as mothers of humanity, women must prevent the genocide across the world, that is to say the depopulation of earth thanks to Covid-19, 5 G, vaccines etc. Women do not harm their children. They love them with all their might, their heart and protect them very jealously, at the cost of their life. Humans need to live in security, in good health, at peace. Here lie mothers duty, mission, happiness, honor and glory. Maternal instinct, intelligence, wisdom and Reason are beneficial and salutary. America is the crossroads of the world. Its women represent all the women in the world. They **embody the strength and courage** needed to save humanity in peril.

Women, take care of your children. Save them. Snatch them from the clutches of ruthless Satanist executioners. Glory is to you! Take control, education and stewardship of earth in your protective, loving and divine hands that give hope. It is your natural and regal duty and mission. It is your prospective and historical responsibility. It is essential to give the political supreme authority to women. It is fundamentally **legitimate and beneficial** for all. This time is too serious. There is no alternative. It is a matter of life or death. God bless women!

CONCLUSION

Here, I appeal to all women around the world and especially the American women about the historical and natural role that they should play in humanity's current life. I mean their prospective responsibility deal with the geopolitical, criminal and satanic current world. I put them face to face with the macabre and very alarming realities of today's world. The whole humanity is evolved in war and terror (bio-terrorism) that reflect the very high level of perversion, of malice, of cruelty, sadism and cynicism of some unimaginable persons and certain peoples. The whole humanity is threatened from **extinction.** I wonder if everyone realizes this. Is everyone aware of the absolute seriousness and of the extreme depth of the current universal evil? It is about **the death of all.** This is **deprivation of freedom and happiness all over the world.** This is unprecedented. It is **the worst** that can exist on earth. It is never known and never experienced on earth before. I wish women were in front row in this global battle. Women are recognized for their bravery, heroism, wisdom, exceptional virtue. Humanity is terribly overdue. It is in mortal danger. It must survive bio-terrorism, as the greatest diabolical plot of Satanists, demons, wizards, eugenicists, racists and mystics.

History of humanity takes a tragic, exceptional and apocalyptic turn. We must awaken all the forces that lie dormant in every positive person in the world and put them at the service of the warlike action that can save humanity. In history of America women give very good lessons that can be used to win this unjust war imposed on humanity by the globalists. American women are incomparable, irreplaceable, unmissable, inescapable in their role as fearless, valiant, heroic and victorious fighters. They eliminated all evils and all the crimes of which they were victims (racism, discrimination, machismo, misogyny, hegemony). They changed the course of American history. From struggle to struggle they came to impose a just and egalitarian sociopolitical order in their country. They have gleaned so many beautiful victories they are enjoying. They conquered freedom, justice, equality, peace, security, happiness, dignity, independence, power, empowerment. All that is due to their character, to their courage and to their extraordinary valor. They are very admirable and very respectable.

So I pay tribute to very deserved American women and I urge all other women over the world to join them to play a very positive role, a very striking and exceptional role in the universal current war.